W9-ANW-377

# THE MOST DOMINANT
# DYNASTIES
# OF ALL TIME

THE LEGENDARY
WORLD OF SPORTS

BY BRIAN TRUSDELL

**SportsZone**
An Imprint of Abdo Publishing | abdopublishing.com

**abdopublishing.com**

Published by Abdo Publishing, a division of ABDO, PO Box 398166, Minneapolis, Minnesota 55439. Copyright © 2016 by Abdo Consulting Group, Inc. International copyrights reserved in all countries. No part of this book may be reproduced in any form without written permission from the publisher. SportsZone™ is a trademark and logo of Abdo Publishing.

Printed in the United States of America, North Mankato, Minnesota
082015
012016

THIS BOOK CONTAINS
RECYCLED MATERIALS

Cover Photo: Mark J. Terrill/AP Images
Interior Photos: Mark J. Terrill/AP Images, 1; AP Images, 4, 6, 9, 10, 13, 16, 19; Vernon Biever/AP Images, 15; DCS/AP Images, 20; NFL Photos/AP Images, 22; Reed Saxon/AP Images, 26; Lennox Mclendon/AP Images, 24; F. Carter Smith/AP Images, 29; Larry MacDougall/AP Images, 30; James Finley/AP Images, 32; Al Messerschmidt/AP Images, 34; Jeff Glidden/AP Images, 36; Mike Derer/AP Images, 38; Mark Humphrey/AP Images, 40; Winslow Townson/AP Images, 44; Elise Amendola/AP Images, 42

Editor: Patrick Donnelly
Series Designer: Nikki Farinella

**Library of Congress Control Number: 2015945546**

**Cataloging-in-Publication Data**
Trusdell, Brian.
 The most dominant dynasties of all time / Brian Trusdell.
   p. cm. -- (The legendary world of sports)
ISBN 978-1-62403-991-1 (lib. bdg.)
Includes bibliographical references and index.
1. Sports--Juvenile literature.  2. Sports rivalries--Juvenile literature.    I. Title.
796--dc23

                                                                  2015945546

# TABLE OF CONTENTS

# 1950s YANKEES
# THE BRONX BOMBERS

The New York Yankees won 27 World Series titles through 2014. That means they have had a few dominant stretches in their history. But they were never more powerful than they were from 1949 to 1953. They won five straight World Series. No team since has won more than three straight.

Hall of Fame manager Casey Stengel took over the Yankees in 1949. He immediately led them to the crown. Over the next five years, his teams included six future Hall of Fame players. They were catcher Yogi Berra, center fielder Joe DiMaggio, pitcher Whitey Ford, outfielder Mickey Mantle, first baseman Johnny Mize, and shortstop Phil Rizzuto.

Yankees catcher Yogi Berra tags out a Philadelphia Phillies base runner during the 1950 World Series.

Yankees sluggers Joe DiMaggio, *left*, and Mickey Mantle were teammates for one season. Here they pose before an exhibition game in 1951.

The team nicknamed "the Bronx Bombers" won at least 95 games in each of the five seasons. And that was when teams played only 154 games per year. Now they play 162 games. The wins did not always come easy. The Yankees played the crosstown Brooklyn Dodgers in the 1952 World Series. Brooklyn took a three-games-to-two lead. But Mantle led the Yankees back. He homered in Game 6 and again in Game 7 to lead the Yankees to victory. Under Stengel, the Yankees went on to win two more World Series before the end of the decade.

## 1930s AND 1990s

The Yankees had two other runs that were almost as impressive. In the late 1930s, first baseman Lou Gehrig, DiMaggio, and catcher Bill Dickey led New York to four straight championships. From 1936 to 1939 the team won at least 99 games each season. Sixty years later, the Yankees were at it again. Manager Joe Torre took over in 1996. They won four of the next five World Series.

# 2

# 1950s CANADIENS
# ROCKET TO SUCCESS

**T**he National Hockey League (NHL) only had six teams for 25 seasons. There was no question which one was the best. The Montreal Canadiens have won 24 Stanley Cups. Ten of those wins came in the "Original Six" era. They won five in a row from 1955–56 to 1959–60.

The Canadiens won 40 of 49 playoff games during that stretch. Former Canadiens left wing Toe Blake was the team's coach. Montreal also had several players who would later be inducted into the Hockey Hall of Fame. The most famous was Maurice Richard. The speedy right wing was nicknamed "the Rocket." He was the first player to score 50 goals in an NHL season. He was also the first to reach 500 career goals.

Canadiens goalie Jacques Plante shows his form in 1958, less than a year before he began wearing a mask.

Richard had a younger and smaller brother named Henri. Fans called him "the Pocket Rocket." The 19-year-old center joined the Canadiens at the start of their five-year run. Many other stars joined the Richard brothers. Among them were right wing Bernie "Boom Boom" Geoffrion, center Jean Béliveau, left wing Dickie Moore, and defenseman Tom Johnson. Some players also were trendsetters. Goalie Jacques Plante broke his nose in a game in 1959. When he returned from the trainer's room, he was wearing a mask. Now all goalies wear masks.

# 3

# 1960s CELTICS

# RED AND RUSSELL REIGN

**C**oach Red Auerbach slowly but surely put together the most dominant team in National Basketball Association (NBA) history. He started as the Boston Celtics' coach in the 1950–51 season. Guard Bob Cousy came on board as a rookie that same year. Another big step happened in 1956. That year Auerbach drafted forward Tommy Heinsohn and guard K. C. Jones. He also traded to get center Bill Russell from the St. Louis Hawks. A year later, he drafted forward Sam Jones. With that, the Celtics had the core of the team that would win the title 10 times in 11 years.

Center Bill Russell, *left*, and coach Red Auerbach were two of the mainstays of the Boston Celtics' dynasty.

The Celtics won eight titles in a row from 1958–59 to 1965–66. They had the NBA's best record in seven of those seasons. Russell won the Most Valuable Player (MVP) Award five times. He led the league in rebounding five times. In his career, he won a record 11 NBA championships. He is tied with Henri Richard of the Montreal Canadiens for the most titles won by a player in North American team sports.

The Celtics did not just win titles. They helped change the NBA. Boston was the first team to start five black players in a game. On December 26, 1964, Willie Naulls replaced an injured Heinsohn in the lineup. He joined Russell, K. C. Jones, Sam Jones, and Satch Sanders on the floor at the opening tip.

Auerbach moved to the front office after the Celtics' eighth title. He named Russell the team's player/coach. The team lost in the conference finals the next year. Then it won the NBA title the next two years. Heinsohn coached the Celtics to two NBA titles in the 1970s. K. C. Jones did the same in the 1980s.

Point guard Bob Cousy was already a star when the Celtics began their championship run.

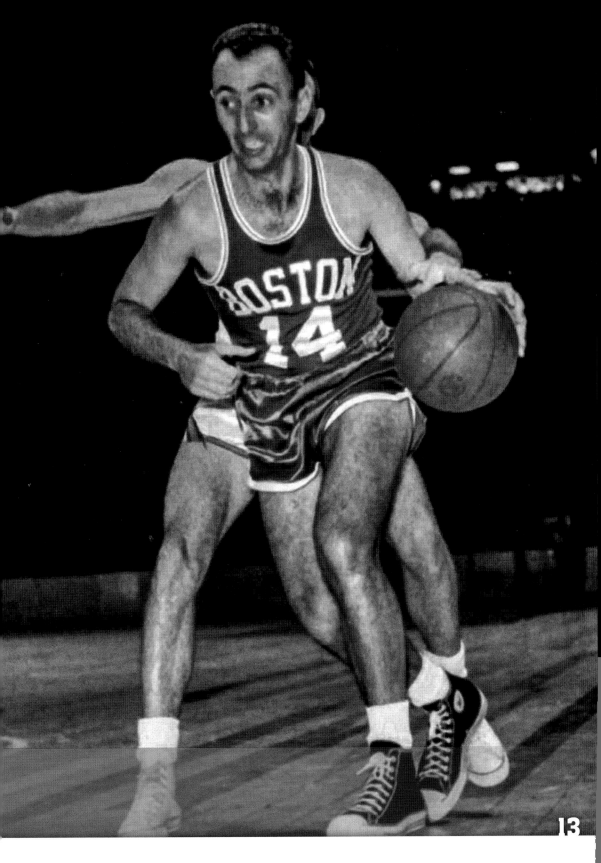

# 4

# 1960s PACKERS
# TITLETOWN

**T**he Green Bay Packers are one of the oldest teams in the National Football League (NFL). The team was named in 1919. Team founder Curly Lambeau worked for the Indian Packing Company. The company paid $500 for new uniforms. Lambeau agreed to name the team for the company.

The Packers won three straight championships between 1929 and 1931. But it was most dominant in the 1960s. Coach Vince Lombardi was hired in 1959. Within two years of his arrival, the team won the NFL championship.

Green Bay went on to win five NFL titles in seven years. Those great teams had many legendary players. Quarterback Bart Starr led the offense. Running backs

Carroll Dale, *84*, Jerry Kramer, *64*, and Fuzzy Thurston, *63*, clear the way for running back Paul Hornung in 1966.

Paul Hornung and Jim Taylor provided plenty of help. Linebacker Ray Nitschke, defensive end Willie Davis, and defensive back Herb Adderley starred on defense.

Lombardi's last two championships came in the first two Super Bowls. Super Bowl II was after the 1967 season. To get to the game, the Packers had to beat the Dallas Cowboys. They met at Lambeau Field on New Year's Eve. The game became known as the Ice Bowl. The temperature was –13 degrees Fahrenheit (–25°C) at kickoff. The Packers won 21–17 on a quarterback sneak by Starr in the final seconds. Later the Super Bowl trophy was named after Lombardi.

# 5

# 1960s–70s UCLA HOOPS
# WESTWOOD WIZARDRY

I n 1963–64 the University of California, Los Angeles (UCLA), men's basketball team went 30–0 and won the national title. That started an amazing streak. UCLA won 10 National Collegiate Athletic Association (NCAA) championships in 12 years. That run included seven straight national titles between 1967 and 1973. No other team has won more than eight since the NCAA tournament began in 1939.

The Bruins went undefeated under coach John Wooden three more times: 1966–67, 1971–72 and 1972–73. In fact, between January 30, 1971, and January 17, 1974, UCLA won a record 88 straight games. The streak started after a loss to Notre Dame.

The undefeated UCLA Bruins celebrate winning the NCAA title on March 21, 1964.

It also ended with a loss to Notre Dame, almost three years later.

Many superstars played for Wooden. Lew Alcindor and Bill Walton were two of the best centers ever to play college basketball. Alcindor later changed his name to Kareem Abdul-Jabbar. Both later won NBA championships and were inducted into the Basketball Hall of Fame. Guard Gail Goodrich and forward Jamaal Wilkes also starred under Wooden. They both won NBA titles and were inducted into the Hall of Fame too.

Wooden was called "the Wizard of Westwood." The UCLA campus is located in the Westwood neighborhood in Los Angeles. Wooden retired in 1975. The Bruins' excellence ended then, too. In the next 40 years, UCLA won the NCAA championship only one more time.

Wooden, known for his work with big men, poses with two of his best—Lew Alcindor, *left*, and Sidney Wicks—in 1969 after UCLA won its third straight NCAA title.

# 6

# 1970s STEELERS
# THE STEEL CURTAIN

**T**he Pittsburgh Steelers were founded in 1933. They did not win an NFL championship for 40 years. Then they won four Super Bowls in six years under coach Chuck Noll.

Those great Steelers teams were known for their defenses. It all began with the defensive line. Tackles "Mean Joe" Greene and Ernie Holmes stuffed the middle. Ends L. C. Greenwood and Dwight White made plays from the edge of the field. Together they were called "the Steel Curtain." The nickname was a play on the term "Iron Curtain." That nickname was used to describe the Soviet Union in those days. Hard-hitting linebackers Jack Lambert and Jack Ham backed up

Linebacker Jack Lambert was one of many fearsome defensive players on the 1970s Pittsburgh Steelers.

Steelers coach Chuck Noll confers with quarterback Terry Bradshaw and wide receivers John Stallworth, *left*, and Lynn Swann in a 1978 game.

the Steel Curtain. Defensive backs Mel Blount and Mike Wagner shut down opposing receivers.

Pittsburgh's offense was not bad either. Quarterback Terry Bradshaw won two Super Bowl

MVP Awards. Franco Harris and Rocky Bleier were hard-driving running backs. The graceful Lynn Swann and athletic John Stallworth were high-flying wide receivers. In all, nine players from that era were inducted into the Pro Football Hall of Fame. So was Noll. He led the Steelers to 13 straight winning seasons and eight consecutive playoff appearances.

## THE IMMACULATE RECEPTION

The Steelers' first playoff victory came in 1972. Pittsburgh trailed Oakland 7–6 with 22 seconds left. The Steelers had the ball near midfield. Bradshaw threw a pass over the middle. After a collision, Harris made a shoestring catch and ran in for a shocking touchdown. It became known as "the Immaculate Reception." Pittsburgh won 13–7.

# 7

# 1980s LAKERS
# SHOWTIME

**L**os Angeles is the center of the entertainment industry. The Lakers were the center of the NBA during the 1980s. The team's entertaining style earned it the nickname "Showtime." The Lakers were a lot of fun to watch. And they won a lot of games. Los Angeles took home the NBA championship five times in nine years during the 1980s.

Veteran center Kareem Abdul-Jabbar and forward Jamaal Wilkes already were in place in the late 1970s. The Lakers added a defensive specialist in guard Michael Cooper in 1978. Then point guard Earvin "Magic" Johnson put them over the top. Los Angeles won the title in 1980. The future looked bright.

Lakers forward James Worthy, *right*, grabs a rebound in the 1988 NBA Finals against the Detroit Pistons.

Guard Magic Johnson helped turn the Showtime Lakers into one of the most glamorous teams in any sport.

But the Lakers were upset in the first round of the 1981 playoffs. Then they started slow the next season. The team fired its coach and hired Pat Riley. With his expensive suits and slicked-back hair, the 36-year-old Riley fit the Showtime image. So did slick forward James Worthy and smooth guard Byron Scott. Soon Johnson was leading the best fast-break offense in the NBA. With so many weapons to choose from, teams did not known who to guard. The Lakers went on to win four more titles by 1988.

Businessman Jerry Buss bought the team in 1979. Many say he was responsible for creating the Lakers' Showtime image. Buss replaced the organist at the home games with a 10-piece band. He also added the Lakers Girls dance team. Lakers games began to attract many Hollywood celebrities to sit courtside. Their most famous fan was Academy Award–winning actor Jack Nicholson.

## MINNEAPOLIS LAKERS

The Lakers did not start in Los Angeles. They began as the Minneapolis Lakers. Minneapolis is known as "the City of Lakes." The Lakers won four of the first five NBA championships, from 1949–50 to 1953–54. Center George Mikan was the league's first star. Poor attendance eventually drove the team to move to Los Angeles in 1960.

# 8

# 1980s CELTICS

# BIRD'S BRILLIANCE

The Boston Celtics had a great run in the 1960s. But they also had a dominant stretch in the 1980s. Hall of Fame coach Red Auerbach had retired. But he still ran the team's front office. That meant he got to pick the team. He did that very well.

First Auerbach drafted forward Larry Bird. Then he landed center Robert Parish and a first-round pick in a trade with the Golden State Warriors. The Celtics used the pick to draft forward Kevin McHale. All three of those players went on to the Basketball Hall of Fame. They also formed the core of a team that would win three NBA titles in six years.

Bird was the Celtics' brightest star. He won three straight NBA MVP Awards. Plus he was a two-time

Boston Celtics forwards Larry Bird, *left*, and Kevin McHale celebrate during the 1986 NBA Finals.

NBA Finals MVP. He and Magic Johnson of the Lakers created a great rivalry as their teams battled for championships. They met in the NBA Finals three times.

Bird had plenty of support. Parish and Cedric Maxwell held down the frontcourt. McHale came off the bench to provide lift on offense and defense. At guard, Nate "Tiny" Archibald ran the point on the 1980–81 championship team. Dennis Johnson arrived in Boston in 1983. He led the Celtics to titles in two of the next three years. Other key figures included guards Gerald Henderson and Danny Ainge and forward Scott Wedman.

# 9

# 1980s OILERS
# THE GREAT ONES

In 1978 the NHL didn't accept players younger than 20 years old. So a 17-year-old named Wayne Gretzky joined a different pro league. Yet after one season, the league folded. Gretzky's team, the Edmonton Oilers, instead joined the NHL. It did not take long for them to find their way to the top.

Hockey was a rough sport in the 1970s. Fighting was common. Many teams tried to beat their opponents through physical intimidation. The Oilers helped move the NHL into a new era. They did not try to out-hit their opponents. They just skated past the bruisers and put the puck in the net. Edmonton won its first Stanley Cup in 1983–84.

Oilers captain Wayne Gretzky and his teammates celebrate their first Stanley Cup victory in 1984.

The Oilers celebrate their fourth Stanley Cup of the decade after defeating the Boston Bruins on May 26, 1988.

Gretzky, Jari Kurri, and Glenn Anderson each scored at least 50 goals that season. No team had ever had three 50-goal scorers. And Edmonton was just getting started. It won four more Stanley Cups through the 1989–90 season.

Six players from the era were inducted into the Hockey Hall of Fame. So was coach and general manager Glen Sather. But the key figure in the Oilers' dynasty was Gretzky. "The Great One" led the NHL in goals five times while he played for Edmonton. He also led the league in assists nine times. He won the Hart Memorial Trophy as the league MVP eight times while playing with the Oilers.

The Oilers had many other stars as well. Paul Coffey went to five All-Star games in seven seasons with Edmonton. He also won the Norris Trophy as the league's best defenseman twice in that span. Grant Fuhr won the Vezina Trophy as the NHL's best goaltender in 1988. He also won at least 11 playoff games four times. Mark Messier was a do-it-all forward. He was the backbone of all five Cup-winning teams. He led the Oilers to their fifth title in 1989–90 after Gretzky had been traded to the Los Angeles Kings.

# 10

# 1990s BULLS
# JORDAN RULES

**M**ichael Jordan is considered one of the greatest players in NBA history. He showed that in his first six years with the Chicago Bulls. He won four scoring titles. He was an All-Star each year. He even led the Bulls to the playoffs in each of those seasons. Yet he and the Bulls could not win the big one.

But help was on its way. Forward Scottie Pippen arrived in 1987. In the next two years, center Bill Cartwright and coach Phil Jackson joined the team. The pieces were in place for an amazing run. The Bulls won six NBA titles in eight years. Jordan led the

Michael Jordan was a high-flying All-Star, but he needed help to become a champion.

The Bulls took a big step forward with the arrival of Scottie Pippen, *right*, and his all-around game.

league in scoring in each of Chicago's championship seasons. He was the league MVP four times.

The Bulls won three straight titles starting with the 1990–91 season. Jordan was the star, but Pippen was a great second option on the wing. Cartwright and forward Horace Grant controlled the inside game. Guard John Paxson was a sharpshooter from long distance.

Jordan then briefly retired from the game after the 1992–93 season. He wanted to play professional baseball. But his baseball career did not last long. Jordan returned for the end of the 1994–95 season.

The Bulls then won three straight titles for a second time. In 1995–96 they broke the NBA record with 72 regular-season wins. That was three more than the previous record, set by the Lakers in 1971–72. The 1995–96 team is considered by many to be the best in NBA history. Pippen was still playing at an All-Star level. New faces included guard Steve Kerr, forwards Toni Kukoč and Dennis Rodman, and center Luc Longley.

## HOUSTON FILLS THE VOID

The Houston Rockets won the NBA championship both years between Chicago's titles. Center Hakeem Olajuwon was named the league MVP in leading Houston to the 1993–94 championship. The next year veteran guard Clyde Drexler joined Olajuwon, guard Vernon Maxwell, and forward Robert Horry to pace the Rockets to a second straight crown.

# 11

# 2000s UCONN HOOPS

# HEROIC HUSKIES

The University of Connecticut was not always known as a women's basketball power. In its first 11 years, the team had only one winning season. Coach Geno Auriemma took over in 1985. He slowly began to build a winning program. Within two seasons, the Huskies had another winning season. In Auriemma's fourth season, UConn qualified for the NCAA tournament. And in 1995 the Huskies won their first NCAA championship.

That title was a sign of things to come. UConn won the women's college title nine times between 2000 and 2015. It set a record by winning 90 straight games between 2008 and 2010. That is the longest

Coach Geno Auriemma talks strategy with Diana Taurasi, one of UConn's many All-Americans.

Maya Moore won two NCAA titles and three Wade Trophies in her four years with the Huskies.

unbeaten streak in college basketball. UCLA holds the men's record with 88 straight wins in the 1970s. Since 2000 the Huskies have gone undefeated over four different seasons. They lost only one game in three other seasons.

UConn has won championships in bunches. It had two "three-peats." That is when a team wins three titles in a row. The first was from 2002 to 2004. Outstanding guard Diana Taurasi led the way. The team had another three-peat from 2013 to 2015. It defeated rival Notre Dame in two of those championship games.

Taurasi was one of many stars in that era. Center Tina Charles and forward Maya Moore led the team to consecutive titles in 2009 and 2010. Moore won the Wade Trophy three straight years. It is given to the best women's college basketball player in the country. Other Huskies to win the Wade Trophy since 2000 include guard Sue Bird (2002), Taurasi (2003), and forward Breanna Stewart (2015).

# THE
# MIGHTY MACS
# OF IMMACULATA

Women's college sports gained popularity in the 1980s. A tiny Catholic school called Immaculata College dominated in the era before then. The Philadelphia-area college won three straight national championships from 1972 to 1974. It appeared in the championship game five straight years and the final four six straight years.

# 12

# 2000s PATRIOTS

# BRADY'S BUNCH

**T**wo games into the 2001 season, the New England Patriots faced a big problem. Quarterback Drew Bledsoe was injured. His backup was an unproven sixth-round draft pick named Tom Brady. But coach Bill Belichick trusted Brady to run his offense. Brady rewarded his coach's faith with a fistful of Super Bowl rings.

Brady and the Patriots won their first title in that 2001 season. They won two more through the 2004 season. And they added a fourth after the 2014 season. The Patriots won at least 10 games in every season but one during that span. They never had a

Kicker Adam Vinatieri blasts a game-tying field goal through a blizzard in a January 2002 playoff game.

Quarterback Tom Brady, *left*, and coach Bill Belichick
celebrate after yet another Patriots victory.

losing record. They missed the playoffs just twice in
those 14 years.

Belichick is known for his great defenses. The early
New England defenses were based around veterans.
Belichick showed a keen eye for talent as he replaced
aging players with new faces every year.

On offense Brady was a three-time Super Bowl MVP. He also was named the NFL MVP twice. He did not always have superstar teammates to work with. But together they always seemed to get the job done. Kicker Adam Vinatieri also was key. He made last-second field goals to win New England's first two Super Bowls.

The Patriots were consistently a good team. However, they had some tough luck in the Super Bowl during that stretch. They went undefeated in the 2007 regular season. Yet in the Super Bowl they lost to the New York Giants. New England went back to the Super Bowl after the 2011 season but lost to the Giants again. The Patriots finally broke that streak by beating the Seattle Seahawks after the 2014 season. That victory gave Belichick his fourth Super Bowl title. It tied him with Chuck Noll for the most by any coach.

# HONORABLE MENTIONS

**Real Madrid 1956-60**—Soccer power won the first five European Cups, the tournament currently known as the UEFA Champions League.

**Miami Dolphins 1971-73**—Played in three straight Super Bowls, winning the final two, and posted the only undefeated regular season and postseason in 1972 under coach Don Shula.

**New York Islanders 1980-83**—Coach Al Arbour led a roster packed with All-Stars to four straight Stanley Cups.

**University of North Carolina women's soccer 1986-94**—Lost only two of 216 games in winning nine straight NCAA titles behind future Women's World Cup heroes Shannon Higgins, Kristine Lilly, Mia Hamm, Tisha Venturini, and coach Anson Dorrance.

**Dallas Cowboys 1992-95**—Won three Super Bowls in four years behind the triple threat of quarterback Troy Aikman, running back Emmitt Smith, and wide receiver Michael Irvin.

**University of Nebraska football 1994-97**—Went 49-2 with three undefeated seasons and three national championships under coach Tom Osborne.

**San Antonio Spurs 2003-07**—Won three NBA titles in five years behind forward Tim Duncan, guards Tony Parker and Manu Ginóbili, and coach Gregg Popovich.

**University of Alabama football 2009-12**—Won three national titles under coach Nick Saban coming out of the grueling Southeast Conference.

**LA Galaxy 2011-14**—Won three Major League Soccer Cups in four years with players such as English midfielder David Beckham, US national team captain Landon Donovan, and Irish star Robbie Keane.

# GLOSSARY

**campus**
The grounds of a school.

**conference**
A group of teams that usually form one half of a league.

**dynasty**
A long stretch of dominance over many years by one team.

**intimidation**
Trying to make another person fear you.

**playoffs**
A set of games after the regular season that decide which team will be the champion.

**rivalry**
An especially fierce competition between two players or teams.

**rookie**
A first-year player.

**undefeated**
Going through a certain set of games without losing.

**upset**
A victory by a team that is expected to lose.

# FOR MORE INFORMATION

## Books

Gilbert, Sara. *The Story of the Green Bay Packers.* Mankato, MN: Creative Education, 2014.

Holmes, Parker. *Lakers vs. Celtics.* New York: PowerKids Press, 2014.

Howell, Brian. *New York Yankees.* Minneapolis, MN: Abdo Publishing, 2015.

## Websites

To learn more about The Legendary World of Sports, visit **booklinks.abdopublishing.com**. These links are routinely monitored and updated to provide the most current information available.

# INDEX

## ABOUT THE AUTHOR

Brian Trusdell has been a sports writer for more than 30 years with the Associated Press and Bloomberg News. He has reported from six Olympics and four World Cups, and he has traveled to every continent except Antarctica. He lives in New Jersey with his wife.